# MAP
## OF THE
# SOUL:
# PERSONA
## OUR MANY FACES

### A Guide

## MURRAY STEIN
in collaboration with
Leonard Cruz and Steven Buser

CHIRON PUBLICATIONS • ASHEVILLE, N.C.

To *BTS*

www.ChironPublications.com

Interior design by Danijela Mijailovic
Cover design by Claudia Sperl
Printed primarily in the United States of America.

ISBN 978-1-63051-720-5 paperback
ISBN 978-1-63051-721-2 hardcover
ISBN 978-1-63051-722-9 electronic
ISBN 978-1-63051-723-6 limited edition
paperback


Library of Congress Cataloging-in-Publication
Data Pending

Special thanks to Carla of the
BTS *ARMY* and to *BTS*
for bringing Jungian psychology
to a new generation.

# Table of Contents

# Preface

## *Persona*

In traditional cultures young people are provided with a *persona* role and asked to fit themselves into it. It's part of initiation into social life. A *persona* requires adaptation to the images offered by family and society, and it tends to stay the same throughout life. If you are a prince or a pauper, you stay in that *persona*. The *persona* places you in a social category–man or woman, aristocrat or plebe, elder brother/sister or younger. Today, however, *persona* formation is often more individualized and therefore more challenging. People have to create a *persona* for themselves, one that fits their specific needs and expresses their individual personality in the present moment. What's more, as a person's needs change and their personality matures, the *persona* must also be modified accordingly. *Persona* management in the modern world is a much more demanding and complex business than it was in the past.

*Persona* is a type of mask. It hides parts of the self that you do not want to be seen by others, and it also express who you feel you are at the present time. *Personas* are created by choosing a particular lifestyle, by clothes, by hairstyle and adornments like jewelry or tattoos or piercings, by cosmetic make up and scent, and by association with friends, a chosen profession or fan club or political party. The *persona* also includes behavior and plays itself out in roles that say who you are for and with others. But it does not say who you are when you are alone. And it is by no means all of you. The "map of the soul" shows a much bigger and more complex territory.

T.S. Eliot, one of the most famous English poets of the 20th Century, wrote that every cat has three names: the name that everybody knows, the name that only the cat's intimate friends and family know, and the name that only the cat knows. When you see a cat sitting by itself and looking into the far distance, what is it doing? It is meditating on the name that only the cat knows, the singular, the unique, the mysterious secret name that remains hidden from everyone else.

As humans, we also have three names: the name that everybody knows, which is the public *persona*; the name of that only your close friends and family know, which is your private *persona*; and the name that only you know, which refers to your deepest self. Many people know the first name, and some people know the second. Do you know your secret name, your individual, singular, unique name? This is a name that was given to you before you were named by your family and by your society. This name is the one that you should never lose or forget. Do you know it? If not, how can you discover it? This treasure may be hard to find. It is the goal of individuation to find it and claim it, and to hold on to it no matter how many times your *persona* may change in the course of your life.

Murray Stein
April 12, 2019, Goldiwil, Switzerland

# An Editors' Introduction
# to the Map of the Soul

When we approached Dr. Stein about putting together a book describing his concept of the inner map of our souls for a new audience of young people interested in discovering the resources of Jungian psychology, we were simultaneously excited and daunted by the project. There is a lot of interest in today's culture about the idea of *Persona* and the psychological mapping of one's inner world. In fact, the interest is so strong that the superstar Korean Pop band, *BTS*, has taken Dr. Stein's concepts and woven them into the title and lyrics of their latest album, *Map of the Soul: Persona*. This surge of energy and interest goes beyond the enormous creativity of the *BTS* members and their huge *ARMY* fan base; it may well be rooted in the collective unconscious that draws primordial energy from the depths of our souls. This book offers a glimpse at some of those energies. It provides an approachable collection of words and images intended to furnish a map of the soul. Any project that sets out to map such a limitless, ephemeral realm as the soul is doomed to failure; however, like the Greek figure Sisyphus, we embark on this seemingly impossible task with a sobriety that this is what writers and publishers do. As Nietzche suggested, it is a matter of *Amor fati*, that is, the capacity to love one's fate even if it means forever starting all over again.

In this introductory section we attempt to draw a rudimentary map of the inner workings of the human psyche. We don't attempt this based on years of psychiatric training, but rather as fellow human beings on the same journey as every person and as followers of the psychology of Carl Jung. We ask your patience as we describe what should remain indescribable.

## The Map

Our map has a center point—actually two center points, the *ego* and the *archetypal Self*. The *archetypal Self* lies at the core of our *ego*. Because it is difficult to depict this idea, we have represented it as a cone through which the ego

Persona

Animus

Anima

External World

Persona

Shadow

Ego

Archetypal Self

C
A

C
A

C
A

Complex

C
A

C
A

Archetypal Core of Complex

Primordial Fire
(deep within collective Unconscious)

Illustration by Steven Buser

funnels into the *archetypal* Self. We will talk more of these structures shortly.

Our map has a large eye looking out towards a village in the upper right hand corner of the map. In actuality the eye gazes outward to the entire world, taking in the totality of what we physically see, hear, smell and touch. It is how our *ego* perceives reality, i.e., through our senses. The eye sits atop a range of mountains that represent the *persona*. The *persona* mountain range sits between the *ego* and the surrounding world. The world can't look in beyond our *persona*, like a high range of mountains that blocks the view of what is beyond. *Persona* is the face, or perhaps better said the *mask*, that we show those around us.

To the far left side of the mountains lies the *shadow* with the ego midway between; it is depicted as a hooded figure. It is no accident that it is directly across from the mountainous *persona* (from the perspective of the *ego*), as the *shadow* is the opposite of the *persona*. Whatever positive face we show the world through our *persona*, a darker and opposite figure forms in our *shadow*. The *shadow* carries all of the unwanted, shameful, unacceptable parts of our psyche. We bury them deep within, hoping they won't be discovered. The *shadow* exists in the unconscious.

In the upper left side of our map and still in the unconscious realm lie the *anima* and *animus*. They are opposite-gendered, unconscious figures in our soul. The masculine figure is depicted as a warrior in this map, with the feminine figure next to him. The classical Jungian view is that a man would have a feminine *anima* connecting him to the deeper levels of his unconscious, while a woman would have a masculine *animus* connecting her to the depths of her unconscious.

Scattered throughout the unconscious lie numerous ovals with a "C" in the middle and a funnel tapering down to a letter "*A*". These are the *complexes* in our unconscious that include an *Archetype* ("*A*") within their core. We will explain these later.

Finally at the bottom of our map we have depicted the flames of the *primordial fire*. This image reminds us that the collective unconscious underlies the entirety of the map. It is here where primitive forces dwell while potent symbols, fears and inspirations gradually emerge.

# The External World

The external world is the easiest part of the map to understand. It represents essentially everything we know as our world and even the universe. It is everything we can touch, see, hear, etc. It is all of the physical world with which we interact including people, objects and other creatures. The reason it is on this map is that it stands in contrast to our internal experience. Our internal experience is harder to grasp particularly as we explore deeper elements within our unconscious —the realm of which we are not usually aware.

# The Ego

The *ego* rests on the surface of the unconscious and occupies the center of consciousness. It is the "I" who speaks, and it is what *I* am aware of when *I* contemplate myself. It lies on the boundary between what we know and what we don't know. It is the "*I*" of myself; what we understand consciously of our experience of being human. It manages and contains, it acts and sets projects in motion, it encompasses traits, characteristics and all the different ways that we "know ourselves." It is informed and affected by all our memories, traumas, emotions, and facts as well as everything we can consciously sense in our bodies. When we have a "flash of insight," it is often the awareness of something unconscious breaking though to our conscious *ego* awareness.

## The Persona

The *persona* is the mountain range (or a mask) that separates our conscious *ego* from the external world and interacts with it. We added an eye between the *ego* and the external world as well to emphasize how we look out from our *ego* into the world. It is through our senses that we perceive the world around us, and this is represented by the eye looking out. What the world sees as they look back at us is our *persona*. Thus, in our map, when friends, family or really anyone looks at us and forms an opinion of us, they are not looking inside our *ego*, but rather at the *persona*, the mask we allow them to see. They see the mountainous exterior of the *persona*. They never see the "true us," only the part of ourselves that the *persona* allows them to see. Our *persona* varies, depending on what role we are in. At work, I might be a doctor. Perhaps I dress the part of a doctor by wearing a white coat or other professional clothes. I use language common to physicians, "doctor talk." I sound professional and may even find myself using big words and professional jargon that reinforces my identity and perhaps convinces me and others of my standing. I may not be as spontaneous with my laughter and I may refrain from horsing around as much as I would when I'm displaying other masks or aspects of my *personas*. This can be adaptive as patients may be reassured by seeing me as a consistent, educated and professional doctor. My work *persona* allows me to function more freely and smoothly in my role. When I go home at night, however, if I were to forget to take off my "doctor *persona*" and not put on my "spouse *persona*," bad things will happen. I might order my spouse around, use wordy or professional jargon, insist on things being done my way, etc. At home, the aspects of my *persona* identified with my doctor *persona* are no longer adaptive; it is actually maladaptive. At home I better put on my "spouse *persona*" or my "father *persona*." With these *personas* I am less professional and tempered. I can laugh, joke and roll around on the floor with my children. There is an endless array of *personas* that we as humans put on in the course of our lives, including those of student, friend, mentor, mentee, athlete, party goer, rock star, social activist, etc.

## The *Shadow*

 Our *shadow* is the contrary image of our *persona*, its opposite. For every aspect of how we try to present ourselves to the world through our *persona*, an opposite part of our personality gets split off and stored in the *shadow*. If I have worked to make my *persona* come across as a friendly, helpful and encouraging person, that means that the opposite of those traits, an unfriendly, unhelpful, discouraging person becomes split off and deposited in my unconscious *shadow*. The intensity of this phenomenon appears to vary in direct proportion with how intense and one-sided my *persona* becomes. A person who presents their *persona* to others as an extremely righteous, pious and devoted person

lacking any anger or negativity is likely creating an unconscious *shadow* with powerful cruel, immoral, and irreverent qualities that can be expected to be just as energetic and forceful but possessed of opposite characteristics. The news has been full of pious preachers speaking out intensely against behaviors they regard as sinful, only to find themselves scandalously caught in those very same actions. One explanation of this is that the more pious their *persona* becomes, the more energized and immoral their *shadow* becomes. Often it is only a matter of time before the unacceptable *shadow* will erupt and become exposed to the public. This can be shocking and humiliating, but it can also be the beginning of a new and more authentic life if handled properly.

Typically, unless we have done a lot of personal work on ourselves, the contents of our *shadow* are hidden and unknown to us. The less we understand about our *shadow* side, the more likely we are to unknowingly act from it and hurt others. It is crucial for us to recognize we have a *shadow* side and take steps to deal with it in healthy ways.

## Anima and Animus

Buried within our unconscious lies another figure that holds the neglected sides of our masculinity or femininity. One hundred years ago as Carl Jung was developing these theories, gender was more rigidly defined within society. It was seldom tolerated in the Victorian age for men to show much of their feminine side or vice versa. Thus, a man who went through life embodying mostly masculine qualities remained unaware of an undeveloped and unconscious feminine figure in his psyche that Jung called the *anima*. It is through the *anima* that a man is able to connect with his softer, more soulful and perhaps more creative side. When he tears up, swells with intense emotions or is more driven by the heart than the head, he is likely connecting to his *anima*. This *anima* might come to him in dreams as a sensual or soulful woman. She is his guide to this deeper place within his personality. She is pregnant with new life, heralding the future.

Traditionally, women had the opposite development in their identity. They were seldom encouraged to follow demanding careers and rarely pursued public roles of power and authority. An unconscious masculine figure typically lived hidden away, a personality with strength and determination and warrior-like power that Jung called the *animus*. In dreams, this figure often comes to women as a powerful male figure. In the second half of a woman's life, she might distance herself from an overly nurturing role and develop a second career with a stronger more forceful and public personality. At such times, her *animus* is surfacing.

This paradigm has shifted dramatically over the last few decades as gender became more fluid within individuals and society in general. Men are no longer forced nearly as much into solely masculine expressions of their personality just as women are allowed more freedom of expression. Nonetheless, whatever gender elements we incline toward, the opposite gender develops unconscious power within our anima/animus. Connecting to those opposite gender traits allows us to become more whole and complete.

## Complexes

Scattered throughout the unconscious zone of our map are numerous *complexes*. We have symbolized them as a "C" within an oval that funnels down towards the letter "*A*". Each one of us has countless *complexes* within our unconscious. A *complex* is a sort of sub-personality with its own set of charged emotions that cluster around certain areas or triggers in our lives, often a trauma. You have probably already heard many of the common complexes that have made their way into our vocabulary such as *mother complex, father complex, money complex, Oedipal Complex, hero complex, Napoleon Complex, Peter Pan complex, lover complex,* etc. Just hearing the title of the complex likely brings to mind a fair amount of what they encompass. Thus, a person gripped by a money complex may irrationally fear poverty and financial need. Even though he has plenty of money, his fear drives him to hoard more and more. One might name it a *Scrooge complex* after the Charles Dickens character in *A Christmas Carol*. Someone who struggles with a *hero complex*, on the other hand, may find themselves irrationally drawn towards rescuing others who may not even need their help. The more powerful a *complex*, the less aware we will be when we fall into it and the more our behavior is controlled by it. Our friends, family and lovers though are painfully aware when we are in the grips of these *complexes*, even as we irrationally defend our behaviors.

A particular point of Jungian psychology is that at the core of every complex lies an *archetype*, in our drawings noted as the letter "*A*". Thus, at the heart of someone's *hero complex* lies the *archetype* of the hero. This archetype is present in hero images known throughout history and embodies all the heroic traits to which humanity has ever been exposed. We can imagine the world's most powerful hero, Hercules for example, lying at the heart of this *complex*. It is that intense energy that a person in the grips of a hero complex is tapping into. These moments can be precarious for those trapped in the complex, or on the other hand, may even result in admirable deeds.

## The Archetypal Self

 Within the framework of Jungian psychology, the *ego* is technically a complex where we hold our conscious self-identity. Remembering that at the core of every *complex* lies an *archetype*, within the core of the *ego complex* lies the *archetypal Self*. By convention we capitalize the *Self* to note its elements of totality and even sacredness, similar to how *God* & *He/His/Him* are capitalized in the Christian scripture. The *Self* is humanity's (as well as each individual's) grand organizing principle. While many have referred to the *archetypal Self* as God, it may be better to think of it as god-like with infinite, boundless possibilities that we often associate with phrases like a *higher power* or a sum of all the conscious and unconscious elements within our universe. It is the *Alpha and the Omega*, the beginning and the end, the *totality* and the *singularity* combined as one. It is hard to write about the *archetypal Self* without lapsing into mysticism and using grandiose metaphors. It is truly ineffable and words fail to capture it.

## The Primordial Fire

 We added the *primordial fire* to the bottom of our map in an effort to show some of the profound archetypal forces underlying these structures. The *primordial fire* represents the initial source of psychic energy and the animating forces throughout human history and even the history of the universe. It drives survival, evolution, creativity and such instincts as sexuality and hunger. When we are

depressed, we have lost contact with the *primordial fire*. When we are manic we may become engulfed in its flames. At times, the fire envelopes the planet, such as during the World Wars or at other times of profound conflict or social upheaval. It has deep veins in the psyche and it runs like lava beneath the crust of the earth, erupting during these intense times.

This is a collective fire that has been burning throughout the ages. Billy Joel's haunting words, "We didn't start the fire, It was always burning since the world's been turning," powerfully capture the metaphor of its ceaseless flames.

So that is our *Map of the Soul*. Before we dive more deeply into the ideas of *Persona*, we thought we would offer a few encouragements that emerge from this map.

## A Few Precepts to Keep in Mind....

### Don't let the world define you. Blaze your own path through!

This is particularly hard for young people. There is so much to do in those early years—excel in high school and college, find the right career, find a life partner, raise children, etc. There is nothing wrong with these things, and indeed many of them are important to pursue, but sometimes these expectations are thrust upon us against our will and they run contrary to our true nature. While the young person will need to pursue some education and vocation, they must do so, however, on their own terms with their own passions and not solely those of parents, friend, teachers or mentors. Looking through the lens of our map, we must be careful that the *persona* we construct retains authenticity; we must listen to our *shadow's* ferocity; we must avoid being ensnared by our *complexes* and we must tap into the inspiration of our *anima/animus*. Only by encompassing this totality, both conscious and unconscious, can we hope to discern our unique path and follow our true self.

## Listen to your nighttime dreams. Keep a dream journal.

A key principle of Jungian psychology is the crucial importance of our dreams during sleep. Dreams bubble up from the collective unconscious and are informed by the *archetypal Self*. All dreams have meaning for us, telling us something we do not yet know but need to know. Write down your nighttime dreams in a journal. Reflect on them the next day and ask yourself what the various elements of the dream remind you of. Avoid the simplicity of a "dream symbol dictionary," as you will need to do the hard work yourself and not rely on someone else's interpretations. If you can, work with a Jungian analyst or other therapist who works with dreams from that perspective. Join or start a dream group where people share and reflect on dreams in a nonjudgmental and noncritical environment. Use your dreams to develop your own personalized *Map of the Soul*.

## Listen to your daytime dreams. Keep a daytime journal.

Consider keeping a daytime journal as well for any thoughts, emotions, creative impulses or inspirations you might have. You can even write out dialogues with other parts of yourself including *shadow* figures, *anima* figures or characters from your nighttime dreams. Ask questions and get to know these interior parts of yourself. Wonder about the present and dream about the future. Remain curious about all elements of yourself, both your interior world as well as how you interact with others. This curiosity will keep you on your path of growth.

## Stay aware of your dark side (your *shadow*). Own it when it flares up and utilize its strength.

Unfortunately, ignoring our dark side is a common trap that we all fall into from time to time. We convince ourselves that we have tamed our inner darkness only to have it reappear after we have ignored it for too long. When our darkness erupts it has free reign to plunge us into various destructive paths. It is vitally important that we stay aware of our *shadow* and the hurtful prejudices, stereotypes and superior attitudes we hold. Stay connected to your *shadow*. Dialogue with it, listen to it, and observe how it is projected onto people and situations in your life, like a movie projected onto a screen. Acknowledge to others when your darker self has taken over and you have done things that you regret. Growth and individuation can only happen if we stay aware of our dark self and are willing to confront our less appealing qualities.

## Stay connected to your body.

Avoid the trap of remaining too much in your head and disconnected from your body and the outside world. This is a trap that many Jungians and other intellectual types fall into. Looking solely at ideas, concepts and archetypes without also looking at how they embody themselves in our physical world can prove to be a costly mistake. Listen to your body. Try to understand when it hurts, grumbles or has a painful memory buried within it. Enjoy your body when it wants to dance, run or play with reckless abandon.

## Stay creative no matter what and express this creativity.

Stay connected to whatever forms of creativity enliven your soul. Expressions are not only works of art like paint on a canvas, but include dance, prose, molding clay, playing music, using your voice, and countless other expressions. Creativity is a great way of tapping into the *primordial energy* in a healthy way that fuels our growth and individuation.

## Know something about your personality make up, its strengths and challenges.

Stay curious about who you are and how your personality challenges and strengthens you. Seek an understanding of Carl Jung's ideas of introversion, extroversion, thinking, feeling, intuition etc. Knowing who we are in these ways and how we engage with important people in our lives not only helps us to understand our behaviors, but helps us optimize how we engage with others.

## Remember the arc of life and that young adulthood, midlife and elder years have very different callings.

It is important to consider where we are in our life's course. In our early years we are typically building our psychic structures, our personality, our desires, our relationships and our vocations. Hopefully we do so with passion and a sense of calling. By midlife we have already built these structures and we may be more occupied with a productive career, a growing family or other challenges. Often in midlife there is a need for a significant course correction. We must stay alert and listen for that. By our elder years we are on the other side of the arc of life, declining in some areas while deepening in others. We are typically exiting careers and mentoring those around us. We are often more spiritual and are nurturing our inner connection to a higher reality. While each of us needs to find our own expressions within these typical patterns, it is helpful to remember that the map serves us differently depending on the stage of our life's journey.

## Remain true to yourself.

Our final encouragement risks being too cliché, yet we feel the need to say it regardless. We must remain true to ourselves! But what does that really mean? Of course it means different things to different people. We would answer the question by saying it involves the vital quest of discovering what your unique call is in this world. It is breaking free of the molds that others attempt to put you in as you claim your unique inheritance as a member of the human race. Whatever your true path is, you must at all cost listen to your gentle, whispering inner voice and honor the signs that life offers you.

Steven Buser, MD
Leonard Cruz, MD
Chiron Publications
Asheville, N.C.

# Chapter 1
# Beginning Thoughts
## Murray Stein

C.G. Jung (1875-1961) was a famous Swiss psychiatrist and psychoanalyst and the founder of Analytical Psychology. After he broke with his teacher, Sigmund Freud, he created his own quite different theory and published many books and papers explaining his views. These have been gathered and published in *The Collected Works of C.G. Jung*, 18 volumes. My earlier book, *Jung's Map of the Soul*, was an introduction to his works and the ideas he put forward in his writings.

I began studying Jung's ideas when I was 24 years old and have been with it ever since. Jung's autobiography, *Memories, Dreams, Reflections*, hooked me and I have never turned back. I find his works as exciting and inspiring as when I first discovered them in 1968. I am a practicing Jungian psychoanalyst and use his ideas every day with my clients. They have not let me down. Jung was a genius of the psyche and his insights into how the human mind is constructed and functions are brilliant. Besides that, they are practical and intended to help people live a fuller, more creative and more authentic life.

# Chapter 2
## *Persona*
### Murray Stein

Two closely-related aspects of ego function are the *persona* and the *shadow*. The *persona* is that face we present to the outside world. James Hall describes it this way:

> "The term *shadow* (...) refers to what is thrown into the "shade" by that which stands in the "light" of consciousness. When something is approaching consciousness from the unconscious, it comes into a field of evaluation that might be called a field of moral choice. Part of what is approaching may be acceptable and incorporated into the ego, with the unacceptable part being dissociated or repressed into the *shadow*.

Contents that are acceptable to the person's ego—that part of us that is "I" and feels itself to be the center of consciousness—are incorporated with little difficulty into the *persona*, particularly if they are also acceptable to the cultural situation in which one exists. The *persona* consists of a "mask," not just in the sense of hiding something but also in the sense of revealing something—a social or cultural role (…) When it "fits well," it enhances and communicates more effectively the true nature of the ego "behind" it; but if it is overused in place of developing an adequate ego, or if used to hide the true nature of the ego, pathologic states occur. Too little development of the *persona* exposes the ego to trauma in a manner analogous to the body having defective coverings of skin.[1]

If you walk toward light you will be illuminated and behind you there appears a *shadow*. A person who becomes too identified with the masks they wear (*persona*) is at risk of having the opposite qualities (*shadow*) overtake them.

"The *persona* is constructed, he [Jung] says, of pieces of the collective that the ego identifies with and that function to facilitate adaptation to the social world around. The *persona* is actually a "segment of the collective psyche," but it mimics individuality. Its existence can be, conscious as a "mask."[2]

"After a certain point in development the human ego and human consciousness become largely defined and shaped by the cultural world in which a person grows up and becomes educated.[3]

"Making such social adjustments for the sake of adaptation creates a social mask, a *'persona,'* that excludes essential parts of oneself. (...) This social dilemma puts a person into what Jung calls a moral conflict. At the deepest level, the imperative is to be whole. Human nature rebels against the strictures of society and culture and if they too severely inhibit this innate drive toward wholeness, and this is a further source of complexes."[4]

"It is not the conflict between the individual and society per se that produces the neurotic problem, as Freud argued, but the moral conflict that comes about in a psyche that wants to deny itself on the one hand but is forced to affirm itself on the other."[5]

*Persona* and *shadow* are virtual opposites. In the early stages of individuation, *shadow* figures often show up in dreams as a same gendered figure whose qualities compensate for the qualities of the *persona*. These can be "negative" if the *persona* is sunny and positive, or they can be "positive" if the *persona* is gloomy and painted with inferior colors.

"Everchanging moral attitudes in our society make it impossible to affirm our wholeness completely in many situations. We have to deny our true feelings (…) to get along or, occasionally, even to survive. Making such social adjustments for the sake of adaptation creates a social mask, a *'persona,'* that excludes essential parts of oneself."[6]

Jung wrote that "Human beings have one faculty which, though it is of the greatest utility for collective purposes, is most pernicious for individuation, and that is the faculty of imitation."[7] Imitation is the basic tool by which we build up a *persona*. We imitate the people we admire and try to look like them. This creates a kind of identity, and this helps us to fit into the group we want to be a part of.

To become fully ourselves, however, we must separate parts of psyche. One place to start is to become conscious of our *shadow* which of course also fosters an awareness of our *persona*. "Actual deep-going psychological separation from an earlier *persona*, and from the sense of identity that goes with it, seems to require both a conscious and an unconscious recognition of the change. When change is acknowledged only superficially, by consciousness alone, but is not also worked through and accepted at the level of the unconscious, corpses tend to end up getting hidden rather than buried."[8]

"The problem of an unresolved and incomplete separation from the earlier *persona* identification is created by a person's natural and wholly understandable desire to deny what has happened and to refuse all terms in dealing with major loss and the changes it portends. This kind of defensive denial of changing conditions, outer and inner, can be overcome only by 'finding the corpse' [metaphorically speaking] and facing death in a concrete and unforgettable, irrevocable way."[9]

"During a period of psychological liminality [a term used to describe a threshold or an in-between state that is often disorienting] socially defined identity becomes a 'mere *persona*,' merely a superficial mask to hide behind or to use for exacting a hollow role in society."[10]

"People do not create their personalities willfully by choosing a specific identity or character any more than they form their physiques by picking out a complexion, a size of foot or hand, or a particular combination of facial features. Neither do human communities develop their cultural preferences and styles in a conscious and rational fashion. Most of what is of individuals and communities comes about through the interplay of historical factors and determinants-time and of origin, genetic and cultural inheritance."[11]

Jung discussed (...), in "The Structure of the Unconscious" (dated 1916), which became the second of the *Two Essays in Analytical Psychology*, and wrote that it is "only the mask worn by the collective psyche, a mask that feigns individuality" (CW 7, §465), he was himself deeply immersed in his own midlife transition and was experiencing intense liminality, as his autobiography testifies.[12]

This separation cannot be completed, moreover, until there is a conscious burial of that earlier identity (or *persona*), in the Jungian vocabulary.[13]

*Persona* is only a hollow mask full of lies and preposterous posturing, to be ridiculed and mocked, as the soul looks out from its position of submersion in the depths of the liminal experience.[14]

In his book, *Understandable Jung: The Personal Side of Jungian Psychology*, Harry Wilmer writes:

"At the border between the inner world and the outer world, is our *persona:* Its face is to the outside, its back side hidden or disguised by the mask on the outside. *Persona* is the symbol of the *archetype* that Jung named for the for the mask worn by the Greek actors: the public expression of face of the part being played. With a *persona*, we present ourselves and our social and external roles. The *persona* is revealed by our faces, our clothes, our body movements, and all the trappings that we use to tell the outer world who we are."

"With our *personas*, we often attempt to present our idealized selves, our *ego-ideals*. Therefore, it hides our *shadows* and protects us from the *shadows* of others. It is a kind of acceptable sham."[15]

The masks we wear are typically fashioned from our personal experience. It starts with the nuclear family, then extends to society beyond the family, and finally reaches out to include the surrounding culture at large. Media assists in this process because by watching characters on TV or in films, for instance, we find resources for *persona* additions and alterations that extend beyond our immediate environment. Whatever serves to extricate a person from their culture and customary environment provides an opportunity to become aware of the *persona*. We become aware of ourselves by seeing that we are different from the strangers around us. That is why travel can be so important. The encounter with an unfamiliar culture permits us to become aware of aspects of ourselves that we see are different from those around us. Also, travel may introduce us to common elements in the human condition by introducing us to people who hope for similar things, struggle with similar problems, fail and succeed in similar ways but who still are significantly different in certain ways.

"Certainly, the experience of separating from an outmoded identity and the requirement of acknowledging the loss of this past self, grieving it, and putting it away are crucial. But this step, which is essentially one of separation from an earlier *persona*, is common to other transitional periods as well."[16]

There is a question about *persona* becoming genetic, as if it is passed down from generation to generation in a family or a culture. Often we can see from the outside that certain families pass character features from grandparents to children to grandchildren. They have significant features in common. They are "chips off the old block," as we say. Although the *persona* does not become genetic in the biological sense, it does get passed down through generations. These are called "memes" sometimes – they are like genetic transmission but not passed on by biological means. Usually people don't know that they have inherited a *persona*. It is as though they live in a windowless room without mirrors. If we are surrounded by people like ourselves, we find it hard to see ourselves in another perspective, that is more objectively.

# Chapter 3
## *Shadow*
### Leonard Cruz & Steven Buser

Our map would be superficial and incomplete if it failed to go beyond the ego and
the masks we wear. The *shadow* is closely
related to the *persona*. When we identify too
zealously with our positive overt qualities
without an accompanying conscious embrace of
the opposite, more disguised qualities we
become subject to what Jung referred to a
"reversal". In a reversal the shadow elements
assert themselves abruptly and unexpectedly.
We must remember that unacknowledged
elements tucked away in the *shadow* tend to
coalesce into a complex that gathers psychic
energy, memories, experiences, perceptions,
biases and more. *Shadow* is a complex, that is
the counter to and opposite of the *persona*.

"Jung spoke of the personal *shadow* as the guardian of the personal unconscious," according to Joseph Henderson.[17] The ego wishes to perceive itself in a positive light. This creates an ego-ideal. Clinging to the ego-ideal brings about and sustains the ego's *shadow*.

### THE THREE FACES OF THE SHADOW

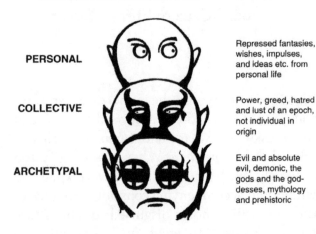

| | | |
|---|---|---|
| **PERSONAL** | | Repressed fantasies, wishes, impulses, and ideas etc. from personal life |
| **COLLECTIVE** | | Power, greed, hatred and lust of an epoch, not individual in origin |
| **ARCHETYPAL** | | Evil and absolute evil, demonic, the gods and the goddesses, mythology and prehistoric |

From Wilmer, Harry. Understandable Jung, Chiron, Asheville, 2014.

Over time as we continue wearing a mask, we become the person we are impersonating. "The *persona* is the guise and manifestation of the role which disguises the personality of the actor. The *persona* is an archetype; it is a functional complex that is necessary for adaptation to interpersonal relations. It is also something we show to others as part of a role we impersonate. It is a compromise between what we wish to be and what the surrounding world will allow us to be."[18] The *persona* conceals our true nature and though it strives to resemble the ego ideal, it is still like putting on a mask or disguise.[19]

According to Robert Johnson, "The *shadow* is that which has not entered adequately into consciousness." He goes on to explain that, "We divide the self into an *ego* and a *shadow* because our culture insists that we behave in a particular manner." [20] The *persona* representing the sum of what we permit the world to see, while the *shadow* comprises the sum of what we cannot consciously embrace.

Regarding the *shadow,* it is as if there is another figure dwelling in our psyche. Jung described a moment when he sensed the presence of another in his dream life.

"Dense fog was flying along every-where. I had my hands cupped around a tiny light which threatened to go out at any moment. Everything depended on my keeping this little light alive. Suddenly I had the feeling that something was coming up behind me. I looked back, and saw a gigantic black figure following.

But at the same moment I was conscious, in spite of my terror, that I must my keep my little light going through night and wind, regardless of the dangers. When I awoke I realized at once that the figure was my own *shadow* on the swirling mists, brought into being by the little light I was carrying. I knew too that this little light was my consciousness, the only light I have."[21]

The shadow is rooted in the personal unconscious (as opposed to the collective unconscious) and it contains all that we "abhor, deny, and repress: power, greed, cruel and murderous thoughts, unacceptable impulses, morally and ethically wrong actions. All the demonic things by which human beings betray their inhumanity to other beings is shadow. Shadow is unconscious; therefore, we encounter our shadow in other people, things and places" and we project our shadow on them. The shadow projections have a fateful consequence for us. What we ignore and project often comes back to bite us.[22]

Our *persona* often identifies with things that are antithetical (opposite) to the *shadow*, or it would be equally accurate to propose that the *shadow* gathers and constellates around principles, memories, beliefs and perceptions that are antithetical to the *persona*. The great danger that the *shadow* ushers in results from the fact that whatever is gathered together within the *complex* of the *shadow* is often projected onto others. Barbara Hannah explains that "Projections isolate us by surrounding us with the veil of delusion that obscures reality entirely. (…) It is a tragedy to see people bring their own lives and other people's to disaster without being able to see how the whole tragedy originates in themselves."[23]

The development of the *shadow* takes place in tandem with the development of the *persona*. Outer influences from family and culture play an important role in this process. A child will be pulled toward family and cultural values and behavior by imitation and will then find an identity in this *persona*. Whatever the family and culture reject and repress will also tend to be rejected and repressed by the child. Gradually, the acceptable things are contained within the *persona* and the rest is contained in the *shadow*.

In later years, an individual may swing to the opposite and identify with the *shadow* features of family and culture and assume a counter-cultural or rebellious *persona*. This then pushes the earlier features previously identified with into the *shadow* and a kind of reversal takes place in the personality. What was previously *shadow* is now *persona* and what was *persona* is now *shadow*.

There is no way to escape having a *shadow*. It is often the case that the greater the *persona* the deeper the *shadow*. Even saints have *shadows*. It's because they are human and have personalities. No one is without *shadow*.

Commonly, a person of the same sex as the dreamer may appear, though they are often not identifiable as a real person. Such a figure that possesses negative or sinister attributes is known as a shadow dream figure.

The *shadow* has been called one's best enemy. Our shadow makes us aware of our dark, hidden side, like a sinister twin or doppelgänger living within us. When a person embraces the existence of the shadow it can become a helpful inner figure. It is important to remember that our failures are necessary for us to become conscious; our failures make us all the more human. The dream shadow mediates between the dream ego and the dark forces of the unconscious.[24]

These reflections on the presence of the gods in our psychopathologies, (…), serve several purposes here. They are a venture in archetypal psychopathology, an attempt to understand, by taking the action of archetypes into account, the psychological dynamics and meaning of pathological behavior. The suffering of the patients who bring these disorders of the soul into the analytic consulting room cannot be grasped without recognizing the archetypal dimension of the unconscious operative in the background.

These thoughts are also aimed at casting some light on how and why the repressed contents of the *shadow* return to consciousness at midlife, particularly during its liminality period.[25] Jung added the following definition of this figure: "By *shadow* I understand the 'negative' side of the personality, the sum of all those hidden unpleasant qualities, the insufficiently developed functions and the contents of the personal unconscious."[26] Jung described this phase of the individuation process as the encounter with the *shadow*.[27]

# Chapter 4
## Ego
### Leonard Cruz & Steven Buser

We commonly associate the ego with the aspect of ourselves that is identified as "I." However, the ego begins to form even before a child begins to refer to itself as I. One can speculate that as the infant begins to recognize the difference between self and non-self the earliest traces of ego begin to coalesce. Referring to the ego Jung wrote, "It forms, as it were, the centre of the field of consciousness."[28] It is "I" when you speak and say, "I am" or "I want" and in itself it is without specific identity. A name lends identity to the "I" so a child named Sara might say "Sara wants" before she says, "I want."

Ego identity extends in many directions, to include nationality, gender, tribe, religion, etc. If a child were not to be given a name it would still have an ego just not a name-identity. It might identify with its family or siblings. First names are fairly recent in human history. Before that an individual simply had a family name and perhaps later might be given a moniker like "big" or "strong." The ego seeks identity and finds it through identification with something like a name or a quality. Ego wants to be distinct. If someone wanted to experiment with the power of the name for anchoring the "I" one could change names and see what aspects of the "I" change. People who have gender changing surgery who also change their names still speak of the same "I" even if the name and the body has changed radically.

The ego is necessary for the evolution of consciousness. At one and the same time, the ego is the subject we want to examine and it is the tool we use to start examining ourselves. Jung devoted significant attention to the ego and in his book *Aion* he makes clear that his concept of self does not replace the ego. For Jung, the self is the whole personality. The ego is not identical with the field of consciousness upon which it rests. However, it does provide a "point of reference" for the field of consciousness and a starting point on the path of self understanding and individuation.

Since it is the point of reference for the field of consciousness, the ego is the subject of all successful attempts at adaptation so far as these are achieved by the will. The ego therefore has a significant part to play in the psychic economy. Its position there is so important that there are good grounds for the prejudice that the ego is the centre of the personality, and that the field of consciousness is the psyche per se.[29]

Were it not for the distortions introduced by the ego, there might be less need to explore the unconscious realms. Jung pointed out that, "It is often tragic to see how blatantly a man bungles his own life and the lives of others yet remains totally incapable of seeing how much the whole tragedy originates in himself, and how he continually feeds it and keeps it going."[30]

One of the first distinctions to make in understanding the map of psychic life is the distinction between conscious and unconscious. Think of the unconscious as the psychic contents that we are unaware of, that we cannot stand to know. What the ego does not tolerate or what it finds unacceptable it represses into the unconscious realms. The ego eventually becomes the storehouse of our ability to recognize our own image and name, as well as our capacity to exercise our will and make decisions. It guides and directs our actions.

The ego displays remarkable continuity over a lifetime. There is great truth behind the poet, William Wordsworth's words, "The child is the father of the man."

In due course, the ego's development is shaped and colored by its encounter with society and culture. The central core of the ego that begins coalescing long before a child is able to say "I," becomes encased in greater and greater degrees of influence by one's ambient culture. Jung described that deeper core of the ego as Personality No.2. The ego that takes on the qualities and characteristics imposed by cultural forces he dubbed Personality No.1. Personality No.1 is shaped by culture and the environment in which the ego unfolds.

Dr. Stein points out that the core of the "I" remains the same from the beginning to the end of life, but its surroundings change over time. Consequently, one's sense of self changes as one develops psychologically. Keep in mind that the *sense of self* is not the same as the self; it is an approximate mirror or aspect of the self. If you become aware of *persona, shadow, anima, animus,* cultural *complexes* and identifications then the sense of self expands and concentrates at the same time. Over our lifetimes, the "I" or the sense of our self becomes like a mandala, a complex image often symbolizing the cosmos or a microcosm of the cosmos, that conveys a sense of wholeness that retains a center. To paraphrase the W.B. Yeats' poem *The Second Coming*, "Things fall apart, the centre **can** hold." In the life of the psyche, the "I" that is the center that does not hold whereas the Self is the archetypal center that does hold.

Recently Dr. Stein was asked for his thoughts on whether or not "the world is a complex," an idea advanced by one of the members of *BTS*. He replied, "We speak of the 'ego complex' in order to put it into a larger perspective of the whole psyche. Often it is taken to be all there is in the psyche. It is in truth only a part— a small part—of the whole. If you say, 'the world is a complex,' I imagine you are doing the same thing— namely, putting your picture of the world into a larger perspective and saying that there is more to reality than you know or can even imagine. This relativizes the term and also shows the limitations of the phrase."

Jung does not separate psyche and soma. They are of the same substance, two sides of one coin. They interact with one another constantly and mutually. The self is a whole made up of body, psyche and spirit. In this sense, Jung was a medical doctor and psychiatrist and so was well acquainted with the close connection between psyche and soma.

Jung held that the ego has some amount of free "surplus" energy at its disposal. This energy is available to be used by the free will and is the energy available to build culture. Most people think they have more free will than they actually possess because they are unconscious of what actually motivates them. At the very least it seems that humans can have the will to live and the will to die. What we do with our free will is very important. All creatures have some amount of consciousness but few species have the ability to will something against what their instincts dictate. Humans seem to be exceptional in this regard.

Dr. Stein was also asked if societies that give importance to people fitting in hamper individuation. He answered this way, "Yes, because the *persona* excludes other possibilities for life and development. But then too much freedom presents other problems. One has to choose a path and follow it. In traditional societies the path is given by social status, class, gender and other things that define a person. In more open societies, individuals are free to find their own path. Sometimes there are too many choices, so many choices in fact that a person doesn't ever get around to making a decision, they stagnate. Individuation needs a certain amount of struggle and conflict between self and society but it must be balanced."

# Chapter 5
# Ego, the Sextant of Psychic Life
## Leonard Cruz & Steven Buser

The ego exists on the surface of psychic life. It encompasses all that is meant when we say "I."

When it comes to navigating our personality, the ego is like a sextant, a tool used by sailors to locate their vessels at sea. When the sun is out the sextant can determine one's latitude by comparing the sun's position to the horizon. Then at night, the sextant uses the angles between celestial objects and the horizon to establish a more complete and accurate location on the earth's surface. Similarly, the understanding we obtain from a purely solar, conscious self-examination (ego and *persona*) is incomplete without the additional understanding obtained through our nighttime and deeper, unconscious explorations. Just like the sextant offers little help in exploring the outer reaches of the universe or the ocean depths and subterranean domains, the ego is poorly equipped to explore the collective unconscious or the personal unconscious.

The aspects of psyche that are conscious are the elements we know, the ones we can readily identify and speak about. The ego is a conscious entity that controls what is allowed to enter consciousness; it keeps unconscious material in abeyance. What the ego determines to be unacceptable, too emotionally charged, too painful to embrace or simply what is inconsistent with its ideal (ego-ideal) is excluded from conscious awareness. The polarization into opposites is what gives rise to the split between *persona* and *shadow*.

There is another polarity related to the ego that is worth mentioning. Jung described the *anima*—the interior feminine figure in a man's psyche—and the *animus*—the interior masculine figure in a woman's psyche. This is "the psychological structure that interfaces with the collective unconscious within, corresponding to the *persona* that interfaces with the collective social world."[31] Jung gave a great deal of importance to becoming acquainted with the *contrasexual* figure (*anima* for men and *animus* for women).

Individuation involves integrating aspects of the *shadow* which opens the door to the personal unconscious and integrating aspects of our *anima/animus* that opens the door to the archetypal, collective unconscious.

> What is it, in the end, that induces a man to go his own way and to rise out of unconscious identity with the mass as out of a swathing mist? (…) It is what is commonly called vocation: an irrational factor that destines a man to emancipate himself from the herd and from its well-worn paths. … Anyone with a vocation hears the voice of the inner man: he is called.[32]

One additional thing deserves to be mentioned. Jung used the term *enantiodromia* to describe the inherent tendency of the psyche to split things into pairs of opposites. "I use the term enantiodromia for the emergence of the unconscious opposite in the course of time. This characteristic phenomenon practically always occurs when an extreme, one-sided tendency dominates conscious life; in time an equally powerful counterposition is built up." At times the ego is capable of "an extreme reversal into its opposite."[33]

A notable example of this is narrated by Marlowe in Joseph Conrad's *The Heart of Darkness*. The narrator recounts how the noble, civilized, idealistic Kurtz undergoes a complete reversal to become a savage, mad, brutal malevolent godlike figure amongst those he would previously have thought to civilize.

The reader will notice that the word psyche and soul are often used interchangeably. This convention reflects that the two words share a close kinship and it serves to remind us to remain humble in our self-examination.

# Chapter 6
# Maps, Perception, & Apperception
## Leonard Cruz & Steven Buser

*The map is not the territory.* (Alfred Korzybski)

"Recently, I was asked about psyche's map. I explained that the map of the soul is a guide to the inner world of dreams, fantasies, emotional reactions and moods, the significance and meaning of attraction and repulsion and the process of psychological development from birth to old age and death. My attempt in this book (*Map of the Soul*, Open Court, 1998) is to help people identify and name what's going on in their psyches when they dream, imagine, react emotionally to other people and change as they age." (Murray Stein responding to a question posed by the *ARMY* fans of *BTS*)

Jung's maps are subtle and suggestive. What they lack in detail, they make up for by pointing out where psychological treasures can be found. Individuation, the process of integrating un-conscious contents into consciousness is like transforming psychological gold from lead.

"Everyone has inner gold. It isn't created, but it does have to be dis-covered. (...) When we awaken to a new possibility in our lives, we often see it first in another person. (...) We project our gold onto someone, and suddenly we're consumed with that person. [and they] appear to be so luminous that he (or she) glows in the dark. (...) When we observe the things we attribute to the other person, we see our own depth and meaning."[34]

The current renewed interest in studying the *persona* has been deeply influenced by a group of seven thoughtful, compassionate young men from Korea (*BTS*). The *persona* is a doorway to deeper encounters with the self. The person who becomes aware of the *persona* and integrates the previously unconscious aspects opens the door to a more authentic full life.

The only tools a person has at their disposal to navigate the interior territory are elements of psychic life itself. Using conscious awareness to examine our *whole* psyche is a bit like trying to look at your own face without a mirror. You may be able to see portions of your nose, lips, eyebrows and cheekbones, but these are a small portion of your entire face.

Jung made clear distinctions between "perception" and "apperception." A perception arises from any of our five senses. A stimulus like a stream of photons (light) or sound waves (hearing) arrives to our eyes or ears respectively. These organs respond to the stimuli and this is what is meant by a perception. In a sense, we all live in a virtual world suffused with our illusions and delusions. An apperception consists of the interpretation given to the stimulus. Although this appears to be a fine point, this subtle distinction keeps us humble. It reminds us that even the best map is still not the territory. An example may help distinguish between perception and apperception.

An emergency vehicle's siren blares out a piercing signal. Let us suppose the sound waves hit two individuals' ears at about the same time. One person jumps out of bed and immediately begins to dress in fire-retardant clothing, puts on a firefighter's helmet and runs toward a fire engine. The other person who happened to be driving past the fire station when the alarm sounds, immediately looks around and experiences a sense of urgency about yielding like the law requires. The sound itself that reaches both people's ears is a perception. The firefighter interprets the alarm as a call to action and embarks on a well-rehearsed routine that readies her to combat a fire or an emergency. The driver feels a very different call to action and immediately looks for a safe way to pull off to the side of the road. They interpret the stimulus differently. Their interpretations of the stimulus were apperceptions.

We form different apperceptions based on a combination of inborn tendencies, life experience, training and acculturation. As a child, perhaps the firefighter was the sort who approached loud noises with curiosity and a desire to explore, while, the driver may have shown a tendency to retreat from novel, intense stimuli. Does this suggest that the firefighter was fated to pursue a career involving rushing into fires and the driver was destined to flee? It's doubtful, but who can say? I wish to make two points. Perceptions and the interpretation of our perceptions are different, and what shapes our interpretations may include our biology, our history, our culture, and more.

# Chapter 7
# Breakthroughs & Midlife
## Leonard Cruz & Steven Buser

Disruptive life events that shatter one's comfortable and familiar sense of "I" often open cracks and crevices in the ego through which the light of unconscious illumination enters. The ego will try to ward off these moments since material that erupts from the unconscious is experienced by the ego as a mortal threat.

There are occasions when the unconscious breaks through and makes its presence known to us. Often these moments of illumination arrive in a tempest of life, a crisis that may be unwelcome at first. Fate often leads a person to a point of opening a crack in their ego , as can intense interactions with others. I see myself one way only to discover that those who know me intimately see something else. In these moments we see there are two strong streams flowing from the ego.

Ingrid Selmer-Larsen, "Janus," c. 1938 (watercolor and graphite on paperboard), National Gallery of Art, Open Access

The *persona* and the *shadow*, like Janus, preside over the transition between what the ego can and cannot endure knowing. Janus was a Roman god who presided over beginnings and ends as well as gates and transitions. He is often depicted with a bust with two faces looking in opposite directions.

Midlife is a transitional time. "It is almost predictable that the repressed *shadow* will return at midlife and particularly during midlife

"Janus," watercolor by Tony Grist,
https://commons.wikimedia.org/wiki/File:Janus.jpg

liminality [a term referring to times of transition]. 'Adolescent' is often the feeling described as accompanying its return: 'I feel like a teenager again.' Perhaps because the structures of defense against the unconscious are less able to hold the repressed contents out, or because the unconscious is more strongly charged with energy than usual and is able to break through them, or a combination of these two reasons, the impulses, drives, fantasies, longings, and wishes that were previously repressed make a powerful reappearance during midlife."[35]

Life's pathways to the future appear to be unmarked and even uncharted, and the future itself seems unimaginable in every conceivable direction. Behind is the period of de-structuring and separation: of general breakdown in *persona* and identity, (...) dreams for the future, and ideals. These have been put away (... [in midlife] ...) Now the way is unfamiliar and ambiguous: collective values, the ideals of youth, old habits do not guide anymore, and there is anxious uncertainty about which direction to take. A person seems to stand perpetually at some inner crossroads, confused and torn. The psychological functions and the attitude that have been guides and counselors in the past are faded voices, and when consulted they do not seem able to persuade very convincingly anymore.[36]

Jung himself experienced the midlife transition as an intense emotional turning point in his life, calling it a "confrontation with the unconscious" (1961, pp. 170-99), and he conceptualized its stages and levels in one of his key psychological works, the much edited and rewritten *Two Essays in Analytical Psychology*. What he describes there is the breakdown of the structure that is the approximate equivalent of what Erik Erikson calls the psychosocial *identity*. This is accompanied by the release of two hitherto repressed and otherwise unconscious elements of the personality: the rejected and inferior person one has always fought becoming (the *shadow)* and behind that the contrasexual "other," whose power one has always, for good reason, denied and evaded (the *animus* for a woman, the *anima* for a man).[37]

From an intrapsychic (interior) point of view, then, what needs to be separated from in the first phase of the midlife transition is an earlier identity, the *persona*.[38]

This mode of functioning comes to serious crisis through the experience of a clear cut defeat, especially if the defeat is large enough and occurs at a critical moment in life, such as the midlife point.

Then a "crack" can open in the identity between the ego and this *persona*, between "who I now feel I am" and "who I have appeared to be in my own eyes and in the eyes of others in the past." The glimpse into this discrepancy can be terrifying. When that former identity and the dreams it was based upon get deflated and lost, there is a sudden realization of the ego's vulnerability and of the *shadow* personality, as well as of the limits on life's ascendance and on its expansive movements forward. (…) This moment of conscious realization is critical for the purpose of separating from a former *persona* identification. Without the full absorption of it, the ego's natural defenses will snap the *persona* back into place and do their best to restore identification with it, even though it may now appear a little false and worn but still, for all its cracks, intact and affording more security than being exposed without it. (…)

A person may experience a critical defeat at midlife, of course, without its resulting in this "full stop" of inventory-taking and conscious separation from an earlier *persona* identification. Terrified at the prospect of facing the future without a familiar persona-linked identity, this man or woman invents the illusion that nothing is actually different. So he (or she) will persevere in holding on to an earlier pattern even after it has effectively undergone demise.[39]

Stein has said in earlier works that, "Complexes are what remain in the psyche after it has digested experience and reconstructed it into inner objects. Analysis tries to uncover the complexes and expose them to the conscious reflection of the ego."[40] Once complexes develop, they shape behavior in ways that are similar to instincts in other species. Like an instinct, we do not consciously recognize the complexes driving our choices, preferences, aversions and behavior. Unlike instincts, they are not inborn and are instead constructed.

According to Jung, complexes are "the actors in our dreams, whom we confront so powerlessly (…) these impish complexes are unteachable." (Jung, CW, Vol 8, par. 202) Complexes prove to be irascible figures that refuse to do what the ego directs. The core of a complex "turns out to be made up of two parts: an image or psychic trace of the originating trauma and an innate (archetypal) piece closely associated to it."[41]

There is an inverse function between the strength of a complex and the ego's freedom to choose its own coure. "The stronger the complex, the more they restrict the ego's freedom of choice."[42]We should note that not all complexes arise from trauma. Jung pointed out that complexes can also arise when one confronts a "moral conflict, which ultimately derives from the apparent impossibility of affirming the whole of one's nature."[43]

"The sociopath is a person without a conscience or a sense of empathy for other people. There is no shame or guilt when they steal from others or wound them. Usually they are people who have not experienced love and acceptance in their lives. Perhaps their parents neglected them or abused them, so they do the same to their children. They can also be very clever in using *personas* that are charming and seductive. There is no inner connection between the mask (*"persona"*) and the selfish ego."

"Like Freudian psychoanalysis, Jungian psychology seeks to overcome repression and raise the *shadow* aspect of the individual personality into consciousness as well as to deconstruct the familiar refrain of the ego as the stable and privileged center of the psychic universe. Pushing beyond psychoanalysis, however, it also seeks to establish ongoing communication with what Jung called the spirit of the collective unconscious. This is a deeper level of soul than the visions of ego psychology reveal. Such a radical move demands arduous psychological labor. Its ultimate goal is awareness and integration of somatic, psychological and spiritual levels of being on individual and collective levels."[44]

"The call to individuation drives us forward and, if successful, releases us from the trap of endlessly repeating the patterns that have conditioned us. The fundamental conviction is that human beings are evolving in consciousness, individually and collectively, and that we can participate in this process and give it energy in quite specific ways if only we know how to do so.

To this end, while I cannot offer recipes, I hope to offer some hints that will be of assistance."[45]

"The task of individuation is to separate the unique personality from the archetypal that often substitute for real individuality."[46]

Individuation "is a project of consciousness-raising and development, to put it in the simplest possible way." This entails forming a conscious relationship to the various aspects of one's personality which is the reverse of further identifying with the most prominent figures in one's psyche and becoming controlled by them.

The individuation process in adults goes forward in two major movements. The first has to do with breaking down unconsciousness through rigorous analysis. The alchemists would have called this *separatio*, the separation of mixed elements. This analytic separation includes dismembering both the identities one has forged with figures and contents that have their primary basis in reality outside of the psyche (i.e., other people and objects) and those that are grounded first and foremost in the psyche itself (the so-called inner figures...). This movement of disidentification brings about the creation of a more lucid consciousness, a clean mirror. The second movement, which comes into play simultaneously, requires paying careful and continuous attention to the emergence of archetypal images of the collective unconscious as these appear in dreams, active

imagination and synchronistic events. This movement involves taking up this new material into the
patterns of conscious functioning and everyday
life. [This is where keeping a daytime and nighttime journal may prove helpful.]

Individuation requires separating the pieces of
the tangled web of motives and part-selves that
constitute our psyche and making the parts more
distinct-in other words, struggling with one's
character and gaining some distance from it. On
the other hand, it calls for allowing newly emergent
features of the psyche to come into consciousness and for integrating them into a new whole. In
short, it means potentially embracing all facets of
the Self with a degree of acceptance and respect.
What Jungian psychology offers is a method for
holding the paradoxes of the psyche in consciousness and coming to terms with its complexity.[47]

"In short, the principle of individuation de-
fines something essential about the human being.
It is an absolutely fundamental drive in the human
subject to distinguish oneself from one's surroundings. This is individuation, at least in part,
and the energy for its creation is a given of human
consciousness. In becoming a person, one must
necessarily create distinctions and separateness.
The drive to create specificity in human consciou-
ness, to become who or what one naturally is, is
grounded in nature. It is in accord with human
nature, therefore, to seek individuation. The move-

ment toward individuation is not optional, not conditional, not subject to vagaries of cultural differences. It is a given, although of course many people ignore it, repress it and distort themselves in convoluted attempts to avoid acknowledging its presence out of fear of appearing nonconformist or being seen as 'different.'"[48]

A single individual whose essential nature is distinctive is moved along by an impulse to become conscious and to become something apart, something unique. In the course of achieving this, a person discovers (or perhaps creates) the paradox of complexity, i.e., the psychological opposites. Contrasting pairs of opposite qualities that contribute to our distinctiveness and pre-ferences also can make a person vulnerable to identification with one or the other in a pair of opposites. The individual person is drawn to identify with one side of the pair and to hold apart from the other. In this fashion, the first stage of definition is achieved, and self and other come into being as a pair of opposites. And *shadow* is created. Here is born, too, the illusion of dis-tinctiveness, for while this is a step in the direction of individuation, it is not yet the genuine thing because the qualities identified with are collective. This is not yet the individual. That is still to emerge. This stage that is identified with the collective, "describes as identity formation during adolescence."[49]

# Chapter 8
# Signs and Symbols
## Leonard Cruz & Steven Buser

Jung emphasized that what a person perceives is limited by the lens through which they perceive things. He distinguished between a perception and an apperception. Our personal history (both conscious and unconscious) along with external cultural influences determine the particular features of the lenses and filters through which our perceptions must pass.

Jung recognized that one powerful way that perceptions are *re-presented* to us is by a sign or symbol. He understood the symbol to be a primary method through which the unconscious communicates. A sign and a symbol differ. Symbols are capable of representing many things at once, whereas signs are more specific in what they signify.

**Signs:**

For example, the Chiron Publication logo is a sign that points very specifically to a company that started in the early 1980s and is currently located in Asheville, North Carolina. The sign is so specific that if someone else were to use it they would infringe on the logo's uniqueness.

**Symbols:**

In contrast, consider this black and white peace symbol. It suggests the idea of peace and also a period of civil protest that arose during the latter part of the Vietnam War. Peace is a multilayered, multifaceted idea. The symbol is more implicit and suggestive than a sign.

If we simply place barbed wire wrapped around the peace symbol then it might suggest struggle or even the recent efforts to fortify our national borders.

The encounter with a sign or a symbol is often more powerful and meaningful than the original perception and certainly more powerful and meaningful than words. There are times when a deep and ancient symbol can be co-opted and be turned into a sign.

 For instance, the symbol of a triangle within a circle is an ancient geometrical figure that suggests many things from the triune nature of the divine to hermetic traditions and much more. It is so widespread as to appear with an all-knowing eye on the currency of the United States of America and is associated with the Rosicrucians.

 That symbol forms the basis of an image that is identified with Alcoholics Anonymous, AA. In having taken a deeply embedded symbol of a triangle within a circle and reducing it to a very specific logo of a particular peer support movement determined to support people in recovery, the symbol became a sign. With this, the mystery, breadth and depth of the symbol is diminished.

Symbols emerge from the unconscious and can be powerful tools in our psychological explorations. Jung viewed dreams as symbolic representations of unconscious contents that have two sources: an outer source in the surrounding world (i.e., the things we perceive), and an inner source in the psychic world of the unconscious. In order to become conscious of the inner, unconscious contents the dreamer is re-presented with symbols. Words fail us! Where our conscious contents and our words fall short, we see that other modes like symbols may deliver.

Music is one of the most evocative experiences and we need only look at the throngs who assemble at concerts for the most popular bands to see the way that unconscious contents can break through and make themselves known to our conscious selves. In fact, the remarkable impact *BTS* is having on its audiences and its *ARMY* fans is inspirational. The band is wedding music with universal messages in ways that Jung recognized as having roots in the collective unconscious. Art, dream images, film and other modalities provide portals through which the unconscious appears to the consciousness. One way to tap into our unconscious contents is to honor and respect our dreams and symbolic experiences. When we learn to recognize symbolic cues we find that art, music, movement, sculpture, and play can all foster the breakthrough of unconscious material into consciousness.

# Chapter 9
# Your Face, Your Name, Your Self
## Leonard Cruz & Steven Buser

"No man, for any considerable period,
can wear one face to himself and another
to the multitude, without finally getting
bewildered as to which may be the true."
(Nathaniel Hawthorne, *The Scarlet Letter*)

We are social beings. Modern researchers
tell us that our speech develops through the
reciprocal back and forth exchange with other
human beings that starts with simple cooing
noises. Facial recognition and discrimination start
at a very early age and even the mask we wear
starts to be crafted when we are quite young.

Converging lines of evidence point to the
fact that ability to recognize faces starts from

birth.[50] Several studies have shown that by 3 months of age, infants show preferences for faces of their own race unless they are exposed to multiple people's faces of other races. This suggests that the face we present to each other and the responses that our faces evoke in one another are among the earliest features of psychological development.

Our face is one of the central components that we associate with our sense of "I." We've learned that people undergoing facial transplants must be prepared for profoundly disorienting experiences when they wake from surgery to a lifetime of looking at someone else's face when they look in the mirror. Experiments conducted using virtual reality technology mounted upon a mannequin and streaming information to the subject has shown that looking back at yourself through such a set up often causes brief periods of disorientation and out of body experiences. Perhaps these things underscore just how much our sense of "I" is bound up with our face.

At the most basic level, when we see our own face in a mirror and light strikes our retina this is a perception. Whereas, the way we interpret what we see is an apperception. On a particular morning we might wake in a despairing mood and the face looking back at us is quite different than on a morning that we wake cheerfully. This is at the heart of what Jung meant to clarify by distinguishing between perception and apperception. The apperception consists of all that we ascribe to a perception.

Our face and identity are deeply related to one another; however, we cannot gaze directly upon our own face. We never truly see ourselves as others see us except on film (even a mirror image is flipped).

Psychologically, we do not see or perceive ourselves the way others see or perceive us. The ego tends to airbrush things. This results in a vast swath of who we are being hidden from view. It should not surprise us that every person seems justified in their own eyes.

What identifies a person includes their physical appearance, their history and the names by which they are known. Dr. Stein using a portion of a poem by T. S. Elliot hints that we have three names. One is private, and known only to us. Even our name has a level that is occult and ineffable. There is more to say about this idea but let's just acknowledge that even something as straightforward as our name is a richly textured, multilayered thing. Yet there are things embedded in our name that remain unconscious to us. So often whatever remains unconscious comes back to us one way or another. This occurs sometimes through fateful consequences.

Jung said, "Until you make the unconscious conscious, it will direct your life and you will call it fate."

Too often a person recognizes after the fact that they unconsciously authored the tragic moments of their life. In part, this results from our inability to objectively and accurately gaze upon our own state, particularly the aspects of our state that are contained in the unconscious. The ego cannot fully gaze at itself.

Jung was acutely aware that our knowledge about consciousness is limited. This is not to say that we cannot be rigorous in our inquiries, but we must accept that we cannot be entirely objective with regard to our own consciousness. Dr. Stein observes that Jung often said that psychology lacks an Archimedean point from which to view the psyche. The Archimedean point is a hypothetical point of view from which an observer can view and perceive something being studied with complete objectivity.

Modern physics has shown us that the act of observation changes the field being observed. We have learned that the observer and the observed cannot be separated.

Late in his career, Jung befriended the physicist Wolfgang Pauli. This may have contributed to

Jung's appreciation for the fundamental impossibility of a completely objective, Archimedean point of reference when dealing with matters of consciousness examining itself. Just like the physicist whose observation alters the field being observed, when we turn our conscious attention to our own psyche, objectivity is lost.

We are limited by our biases. We are look at ourselves but not from an outside perspective. Maybe extraterrestrials could tell us more about our psyches precisely because they would have an external point of comparison.

# Chapter 10
## Personal and Collective Unconscious
### Leonard Cruz

Some things exist on the very edge of awareness and easily breakthrough. I briefly forget
where I place my car keys and with a little effort
I remember. These moments prove there is a
region of the unconscious beyond our immediate
awareness but not entirely inaccessible. This
region of the unconscious is seldom revelatory.

On the other hand, deeper and more
inaccessible regions of the unconscious exist
that prove more difficult to recover. These are
typically more emotionally charged and meaningful. Early in his career, Jung conducted word
association experiments in which he measured
subject's emotional responses to words presented
to them. He discovered that some words elicited

a significant emotional charge for a person and that these groups of words are often associated with traumatic memories. This was his earliest encounter with *complexes*.

Jung found some evidence that *complexes* were shared between mothers and daughters and fathers and sons. Cultural complexes also get passed on to the new generation. Partly this is because we are great imitators. We may become aware of the grip our cultural *complexes* have over us, especially when we encounter others from different cultures who react differently. People from different cultures do not share our *complexes*. Jung's Word Association Experiments were conducted at about the same time that Sigmund Freud, the great Austrian psychiatrist who pioneered the field of psychoanalysis, was advancing the idea that psychological afflictions resulted from repressed childhood memories that were traumatic or unacceptable. Freud celebrated Jung's experimental evidence since it confirmed the existence of unconscious forces that influence behavior.

Eventually, Jung and Freud broke with each other in part because Jung's understanding of the unconscious went far beyond the goal of identifying and treating pathological states. Jung regarded the unconscious as a vast repository of our personal (sometimes traumatic) past as well as collective unconscious contents that are shared by large groups of people within a culture or among the entire human race. Within this vast storehouse exist recurring unconscious patterns, like engrams, that appear in the motifs of fairy tales, myths, art, movies and more.

Collective unconscious elements are embedded in the deepest layers of our psyche. Though they may be apparent within a culture, any single member of a culture may struggle to identify the collective unconscious elements influencing their own lives. In part, this is because we cannot easily separate ourselves from the culture in which we arise. Expecting a person to recognize the collective unconscious influences in their life is like asking a fish to describe what it's like to live in water; it is all that we know.

# Chapter 11
# Individuation: Finding your Path
## Leonard Cruz & Steven Buser

One of Jung's great gifts to future explorers was the map he left behind of the unconscious domains. Through his own courageous explorations, he marked out structures like complexes, archetypes and symbols that serve the serious psychological explorer well.

In order to explore the inner landscape, the ego must be carried along reluctantly. Every person must eventually get around to developing a map of the soul (psyche) that is their own. Such a map will have a great deal in common with others. Every person must undertake a highly individualized journey and explore the territory of the psyche for themselves. This requires us to turn away from the chatter of our times, our culture, and sometimes even our families of origin in order to hear the call to an individual path. Jung referred to the path that is unique to each of us as individuation.

"The act of consciousness is central; otherwise we are overrun by the complexes. The hero in each of us is required to answer the call of individuation. We must turn away from the cacophony of the outer world to hear the inner voice. When we can dare to live its promptings, then we achieve personhood. We may become strangers to those who thought they knew us, but at least we are no longer strangers to ourselves."[51]

*BTS* started a campaign encouraging fans with "Love myself." They suggest their fans stop comparing themselves to others, that they find something they want to do and make it their own, and that they discover themselves while reading a book. *BTS* is offering its own strategy for mapping the soul. James Hollis, an American Jungian analyst, explains that "The paradox of individuation is that we best serve intimate relationship by becoming sufficiently developed in ourselves that we do not need to feed off others."[52]

Jung wrote, "What is it, in the end, that induces a man to go his own way and to rise out of unconscious identity with the mass as out of a swathing mist? (...) It is what is commonly called vocation: an irrational factor that destines a man to emancipate himself from the herd and from its well-worn paths. ... Anyone with a vocation hears the voice of the inner man: he is called."[53]

# Chapter 12
# Complexes
## Murray Stein

A centerpiece of Jung's psychology is the *complex*. A *complex* is an unconscious pattern of perceptions, emotions and memories organized around a common theme or an archetype. Early in Jung's career he conducted experimental trials looking for emotional reactions to words. He discovered that certain words were associated with strong emotional reactions. His subjects recounted that the group of words that evoked responses were associated with emotionally charged memories, often traumatic memories. This discovery convinced the young psychiatrist that unconscious forces were at play. He came to the conclusion that there were *complexes* in the psyche that coalesced memories, perceptions, and energy. His ideas about the central role played by *complexes* changed very little during the remainder of Jung's career. *Complexes* are like building blocks of the psyche. Because *complexes* operate in autonomous ways, they tend to interfere with the exercise of one's will. The complexes also distort emotions and memories.

Others had written about *complexes* before Jung made his contributions to this area of study. Freud and some of his followers had popularized ideas like the Oedipal Complex and the Inferiority Complex, but Jung went one step further. He proposed that our personality is made up of numerous *complexes* that function in semi-autonomous fashion like little subpersonalities. Some *complexes* might be rooted more in one's personal unconscious whereas other *complexes* might be rooted more in the collective unconscious.

A *complex* exerts powerful influence over a person. They gather to themselves a tremendous amount of energy and becomes storehouses for our own *memories, dreams and reflections*. How can a person control the effect exerted by *complexes*?

Certainly, therapy and analysis strive to loosen the grip *complexes* exert over us. As the elements of the unconscious breakthrough to consciousness, we can work through both the personal and collective levels of unconscious material. This permits a person to begin constructing their own *map of the soul*. This often starts with the dim awareness of the *persona* from which we can become disentangled. This inquiry, this royal road that leads to individuation is best approached with a certain degree of fearlessness and a large dose of self-love.

We must not lose sight of the fact that we are continually adding material to the *complex* throughout our life. Memories, perceptions and experience are encountered through the lenses of our complexes. Moments of "enlightenment" in which all of the material attached to complexes is put aside and transcended do occur. These can become transformative experiences, particularly if we have spent time preparing for such encounters with the soul. However, normal consciousness inevitably returns and the struggle to be aware of the influence exerted by our *complexes* continues. While therapy or analysis intends to bring unconscious material into the light of consciousness, the ego in league with the *persona* prove to be formidable opponents to this effort.

The person who comes to believe they have forever left behind personal and collective *complexes* is living an illusion, personal and collective *complexes* and archetypal and cultural influences are simply not behind once and for all. Anyone who falls victim to such folly can be said to have suffered *inflation*, a rather unhealthy and even dangerous mental state in which one's ego becomes identified with the larger Self that is the whole of our conscious and unconscious psyche.

I was recently asked to speculate on the effect that chronic, neurodegenerative diseases like Alzheimer's Disease or Chronic Traumatic Encephalopathy resulting from repeated blows to the head might have upon the *complexes*. I suppose that even when memory has been lost or obliterated, the unconscious *complex* can continue operating, and these can induce irrational behaviors. In such conditions, the rational mind supported by memory weakens or becomes entirely absent, but the instinctive and irrational mind remains. This is simply a guess as to how such pathological processes exert an impact on the complexes.

# Chapter 13
# Love Yourself, Know Your Name, Speak Yourself
## Leonard Cruz

The process of individuation involves communicating with and befriending the interior figures who appear. The use of active imagination (a practice of conversing with our interior figures) painting and other creative arts, sand play therapy and journaling are among the tools that help a person bring the unconscious to consciousness.

Revealing one's true self can feel incredibly dangerous. There is the risk of being rejected, ostracized, and cast out. Each compromise we make in an effort to adapt to society risks betraying our authentic self. The mask one wears forms with each accommodation one makes. The person who becomes over identified with the mask they wear becomes distant from the authentic aspects of psyche. Lucky is the person whose *persona* begins to  disintegrate.

In the movie, *Spider Man 3*, the main character comes into contact with a material that arrives on earth in a meteor. The material has a sort of symbiotic quality that brings out the negative aspects of Spider Man. It brings out his shadow side. Dressed in a black Spider Man outfit, this shadow Spider Man acts with revenge, he is unrestrained in his violence, he even kills. The drama erupts when Peter Parker, the non-super hero person who is also Spider Man, confronts his shadow side. The real victory is when he deals with his darker side.

If you identify strongly with a *persona* after a time you will feel only what the *persona* allows. This gives you strength in some situations to ignore distracting emotions or attacks, but it can also prevent you from thinking in original ways. The *persona* restricts thinking and feeling, particularly if the mask is too tightly glued to the actor's face. He or she may be a good actor in that specific role but they will be out of touch when the situation changes, and the mask no longer fits well into the frame.

When the *persona* starts to disintegrate the process of individuation is accelerated. The *persona* is a necessary psychic element and its disintegration is likely to feel threatening. It must be remembered that hiding our true nature behind the mask—the *persona*—produces insidious, malignant effects. The disintegration of the *persona* catalyzes the process of individuation.

Remember that whatever appears in the psychic life is considered to be part of the entire *self*. To really love yourself you must love ALL of your *self*. If you only love your ego you miss out on the wonderous totality of who you are. This will also make you less able to love the world. The parts of your *self* that you fail to love or worse yet the parts you scorn are apt to be projected onto others. In its extreme this can provoke hatred toward the world and others. Few people who act with brutality and malevolence perceive themselves accurately. The phrase *haters gonna hate*, a phrase popularized by Taylor Swift in her song *Shake it Off*, comes to mind.

As RM from *BTS* said in his address to the United Nations, "Love yourself, love the world, know your name."

"So, let's all take one more step. We have learned to love ourselves, so now I urge you to speak yourself. I would like to ask all of you. What is your name? What excites you and makes your heart beat?

Tell me your story. I want to hear your voice, and I want to hear your conviction. No matter who you are, where you're from, your skin color, gender identity: speak yourself. Find your name, find your voice by speaking yourself.

I'm Kim Nam Jun, RM of *BTS*. I'm a hip-hop idol and an artist from a small town in Korea."

I want to return to the ideas Dr. Stein put forth in his reference to T.S. Elliott's poem "The Naming of Cats." Our given name, the one by which most people know us, is deeply embedded. This is a name that we grow into and it is mostly imposed on us. Gradually, we connect "I" with our given name. While a name change disengages a person from their given name such a person's sense of "I" may not change much and there will often be others who continue to know the person by their given name. For example, at age 23, I met my wife who began to call me Len and this replaced my given name of Leonard or my nickname Lenny, except among those who only knew me before I met my wife.

There is a name that our intimates know. This is often a nickname or an endearing name like Boo or Sweetie. Even a name given by a bully is one that requires a certain degree of intimate connection. If a coworker were to address us by the intimate name a spouse uses, it would surprise or dismay us. This reveals that our second name is one reserved for a small group of individuals, the inner circle of our acquaintances. As time goes by, we also grow into our second name. The first time your girlfriend calls you "Sweetie" may stir a different effect than when she utters the same name after decades of marriage in which you've shared countless joys and sorrows.

Finally, there is a name that only we know. It is a reflection of our private-most self. This private name is often uttered in the regions of liminality, the in between realms. The one who is called by that name often is called by other voices, ephemeral figures not unlike Philemon who visited Jung, and synchronistic moments that beckon to us from the deep.

When we are in touch with the ethereal realm, even inanimate objects seem to speak with a universal voice. For some people, the spirit of the depths calls out from the rocks, the trees, a book, or a song.

I love books and have often sensed that a book speaks to me. One of my daughters is an avid rock climber and I believe I have seen her commune with a rock wall while my other daughter loves to dance and seems to gain deep impressions when she dances or listens to music.

RM of *BTS* urges his fans: "Know your name." This is every person's challenge.

The deepest name is the name that only we know and that sometimes even with our best effort is hard to retrieve. So much of who we are remains unconscious, and this requires lifelong, painstaking work to uncover and integrate into consciousness.

Among Orthodox Jews great care is taken to never write or utter God's true name. YHWH is used in place of YAHWEH out of a sign of deep reverence and recognition that to use God's name would be to reduce God. Augustine of Hippo said, "If you understand, then it is not God." Perhaps our third name is similar to the reverent way that Jewish people refer to God by removing vowels from the name leaving a symbol in its place.

To reach the place where our true name is found we must shake off the effects of our upbringing. We must release the fear and caution that arises from repeated hurts and wounds. We must cast off the shame associated with our mistakes. Most of all, we must recognize and free ourselves from cultural constraints. Those who accomplish this last task will be better prepared to honor our shared humanity. If you hope to live authentically, you must search for your deepest, truest name.

# Afterword
## Murray Stein

*Everything now depends on man.*
(Jung, *Answer to Job, par. 675*)

I first learned about the interest that *BTS* had in my work from a Japanese student at the International School of Analytical Psychology in Zurich. I was pleasantly surprised to hear that my earlier book, *Jung's Map of the Soul,* was being recommended on the *BTS's* website. Later when this same student informed me that the new *BTS* album was titled, "Map of the Soul: Persona," I was bowled over. This also inspired me to write a short book of the same title in which I could present many of the ideas I have worked with for decades. It's taken me a while to get used to the idea. I still don't know what it means but I believe it will be enormously helpful in introducing others to the profound insights that Jung gave us. I am especially happy that Jung's ideas are being popularized among younger people. The possibility that younger folks will seriously explore these themes and give attention to living more authentically, loving themselves and thereby create a more loving world is heartening.

I have begun to listen to and study some of the earlier works of *BTS*. They strike me as a serious, thoughtful group of young people dedicated to the noble cause of raising consciousness, preventing mobbing, increasing self-acceptance and fighting the plague of suicide that besets so many parts of the world today especially among young people. They are saying that life is worth living. I support this with all my heart. And maybe *Map of the Soul: Persona* will help support these worthy efforts.

*BTS* has a message. Many pop artists also carry a message but often it's more about anger and outrage than about consciousness, identity, love and such positive psychological developments. The *ARMY* fan base seems extremely dedicated and extremely respectful.

I confess to being enchanted by the way that *BTS* has used various books like *Demian, The Ones Who Walk Away from Omelas*, and *Into the Magic Shop* to weave complex tales full of symbolism. The band's ability to use one creative work to inspire their creative musical endeavors is fascinating. It may interest the *ARMY* fans to know that Dr. Jung was a man who sculpted, built a tower to which he retreated, and composed a book called *The Red Book* in which he placed astonishing hand-painted color plates and calligraphy. It is often a sign of psychological depth and flexibility to be able to be creative and even more so to create in various genres.

I don't know if attending some *BTS* concerts might help me understand why their message has been so influential. I suspect that *BTS* communicates with their fans on many levels, some of them quite non-rational. Symbols are always more than rational, and they engage our attention in ways that we can't explain. We can only reflect on the effect symbols have on us and try to understand how they are moving us.

Jung is still relevant today, perhaps more relevant than ever. The value of Jung's theories has only increased with time as people have tested them and used them in new ways. Today Jungian psychoanalysts are located on every inhabited continent, and study groups and training programs can be found all around the world. In Korea, for instance, Prof. Bou-Yong Rhi brought his Jungian training that he received in Zurich, Switzerland to Seoul in the mid 1960's.

He has been responsible for introducing Jung's ideas to the Korean audience by translating many of his works and teaching new generations of psychiatrists at the University.

The Jungian movement continues to grow worldwide and especially rapidly in areas of the world that were not exposed to Jung's ideas before the end of the Cold War in 1990. There have been hundreds of contributors to the field of Analytical Psychology since Jung's time, and Jungian publications continue pouring out of publishing houses in many languages. I am very happy to say that Jungian psychology has a very bright future in this century and beyond.[54]

"As one becomes a good citizen, a devoted son or daughter, a dedicated member of church, school, and state, a reliable employee, a husband or wife, a father or mother, an ethical professional, people feel confident that they can trust such a person and therefore give her or him their high esteem. Such persons speak clearly for family, community, nation or even for all of humanity, but not for themselves. If individuals who have adopted such faithful and steady personae remain unconscious of their true individuality, that individuality remains undiscovered, and they become a mere mouthpiece for the collective attitudes that they have become identified with. While this may serve a person's interests to a point-because everyone after all has to adapt to society and culture; and because a well-constructed *persona* is a distinct advantage for practical purposes of survival and social success this is clearly not the goal of individuation. It is only a staging point for beginning the individuation process.

Understandably enough, people are tempted to stop here, since creating a smooth and well-functioning *persona* is not such an easy thing. If identification with the personal elements that make up the *persona* is an impediment to individuation on the one hand, identification with archetypal figures of the collective unconscious is another and perhaps even more difficult (because more subtle) obstacle to be overcome."[55]

Mario Jacoby, a renowned Jungian analyst wrote that "A strong ego relates to the outside world through a flexible *persona*; identifications with a specific *persona* (doctor, scholar, artist, etc.) inhibits psychological development."[56]

2019

# Endnotes

[1] Hall, James A., *The Jungian Experience: Analysis and Individuation*, InnerCity, Toronto, 1986, p 19.

[2] Stein, Murray, *The Principles of Individuation*, Chiron Publications, Asheville, 2015, p 11.

[3] Stein, Murray, *Jung's Map of the Soul*, Open Court, Peru, IL, 1998, p22.

[4] (Ibid, p 56)

[5] (Ibid, p 55)

[6] (Ibid, p54)

[7] "The Structure of the Unconscious" *CW*, vol. 7, Par

[8] Stein, Murray, *In Midlife: A Jungian Perspective*, Chiron Publications, Asheville, 2014, p 38.

[9] Stein, Murray *In Midlife: A Jungian Perspective*, Chiron, Asheville, p 35.

[10] (Ibid, p 117)

[11] Stein, Murray, *The Principles of Individuation*, Chiron Publications, Asheville, 2015, p iv

[12] (Ibid, 56)

[13] (Ibid, p 41)

[14] (Ibid, p 56)

[15] Wilmer, Harry, *Understandable Jung: The Personal Side of Jung Psychology*, Chiron, 2014, p 33.

[16] (Ibid, 109)

[17] Henderson, Joseph, *Shadow and Self*, Chiron, 1990, p 64.

[18] Wilmer, Harry *Practical Jung, p 65*

[19] (Ibid, p 67)

[20] Johnson, Robert, *Owning Your Shadow*, HarperCollins, 1993, p 4.

[21] Jung, *Memories, Dreams, Reflections*, Vintage, Ney York, 1965, p 88

[22] Wilmer, Harry, *Practical Jung*, Chiron, *p 96.*

[23] Hannah, Barbara, *Lectures on Jung's Aion*, Chiron, 2008, p 18.

[24] Wilmer, Harry, *Practical Jung*, Chiron, *p 109*

[25] Stein, Murray *In Midlife: A Jungian Perspective*, Chiron, Asheville, p 78.

[26] Jung, *CW* 9, p103.

[27] (Ibid, p 13-19)

[28] Jung, CW Vol 9/11. Par. 1.

[29] Jung, CW Vol 9/11 par. 11.

[30] Jung, CW Vol 9/11 par

[31] (Ibid, p 17)

[32] Jung, CG, *The Development of Personality*, CW. Vol 29, p 299-300.

[33] Jung, CG, *The Question of Psychological Types: The Correspondence of* C. G. *Jung and Hans Schmid-Guisan*

[34] Johnson, Robert, *Inner Gold*, Koa Books, 2008.

[35] Stein, Murray, *The Principles of Individuation*, Chiron Publications, Asheville, 2015, p 76.

[36] Stein, Murray, *In Midlife: A Jungian Perspective*, Chiron Publications, Asheville, 2014, p 85-86.

[37] Stein, Murray, *In Midlife: A Jungian Perspective*, Chiron Publications, Asheville, 2014, p 26.

[38] (Ibid, p 27)

[39] (Ibid, p 33-34)

[40] Stein, Murray, *Jung's Map of the Soul*, Open Court, Asheville, p 49.

[41] Stein, Murray, *Jung's Map of the Soul*, Open Court, Asheville, p52.

[42] (Ibid, p 52)

[43] Jung, *CW,* Vol 8, par. 204.

[44] (Ibid)

[45] (Ibid, p *xvii)*

[46] (Ibid, p 17)

[47] Stein, Murray, *The Principles of Individuation*, Chiron Publications, Asheville, 2015, p 4-6.

[48] Stein, Murray, *The Principles of Individuation*, Chiron Publications, Asheville, 2015, p 8.

[49] Stein, Murray, *The Principles of Individuation*, Chiron Publications, Asheville, 2015, p 9-10.

[50] Otsuka, Y, Face Recognition in Infants: A review of behavioural and near-infrared spectroscopic studies, *Japanese Psychological Research*, 2014, Volume 56 No. 1, 76-90.

[51] Hollis, James, *The Middle Passage*, InnerCity, Toronto, 116.

[52] (Ibid, p. 95)

[53] Jung, *The Development of Personality*, Para 299-300.

[54] Interview with Laura London in answer to questions presented by *BTS* related to *Jung's Map of the Soul*, Open Court, Peru IL, 1998.

[55] Stein, Murray, *The Principles of Individuation*, Chiron Publications, Asheville, 2015, p 13-15.

[56] Jacoby, Mario, *The Analytic Encounter*, InnerCity, Toronto, 1984, p 118.